MOVIE HITS FOR THE TEEN PLAYER

EASY PIANO ARRANGEMENTS BY DAN COATES

Project Manager: Carol Cuellar
Art Layout: Joe Klucar

DAN COATES® is a registered trademark of Warner Bros. Publications

Dan Coates

As a student at the University of Miami, Dan Coates paid his tuition by playing the piano at south Florida nightclubs and restaurants. One evening in 1975, after Dan had worked his unique brand of magic on the ivories, a stranger from the music field walked up and told him that he should put his inspired piano arrangements down on paper so they could be published.

Dan took the stranger's advice—and the world of music has become much richer as a result. Since that chance encounter long ago, Dan has gone on to achieve international acclaim for his brilliant piano arrangements. His Big Note, Easy Piano and Professional Touch arrangements have inspired countless piano students and established themselves as classics against which all other works must be measured.

Enjoying an exclusive association with Warner Bros. Publications since 1982, Dan has demonstrated a unique gift for writing arrangements intended for students of every level, from beginner to advanced. Dan never fails to bring a fresh and original approach to his work. Pushing his own creative boundaries with each new manuscript, he writes material that is musically exciting and educationally sound.

From the very beginning of his musical life, Dan has always been eager to seek new challenges. As a five-year-old in Syracuse, New York, he used to sneak into the home of his neighbors to play their piano. Blessed with an amazing ear for music, Dan was able to imitate the melodies of songs he had heard on the radio. Finally, his neighbors convinced his parents to buy Dan his own piano. At that point, there was no stopping his musical development. Dan won a prestigious New York State competition for music composers at the age of 15. Then, after graduating from high school, he toured the world as an arranger and pianist with the group Up With People.

Later, Dan studied piano at the University of Miami with the legendary Ivan Davis, developing his natural abilities to stylize music on the keyboard. Continuing to perform professionally during and after his college years, Dan has played the piano on national television and at the 1984 Summer Olympics in Los Angeles. He has also accompanied recording artists as diverse as Dusty Springfield and Charlotte Rae.

During his long and prolific association with Warner Bros. Publications, Dan has written many award-winning books. He conducts piano workshops worldwide, demonstrating his famous arrangements with a special spark that never fails to inspire students and teachers alike.

CONTENTS

ACROSS THE STARS
(LOVE THEME FROM *STAR WARS*®: EPISODE II)

Music by
JOHN WILLIAMS
Arranged by DAN COATES

Gently (♩ = 76)

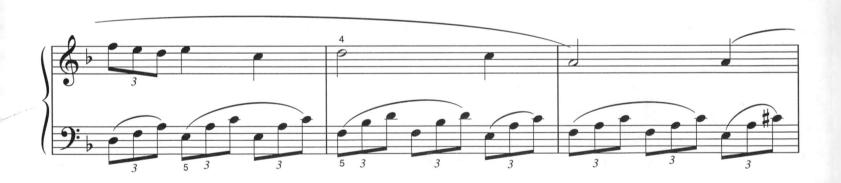

Appassionato

ANGEL EYES

Words and Music by
MIKE CURB and MICHAEL LLOYD
Arranged by DAN COATES

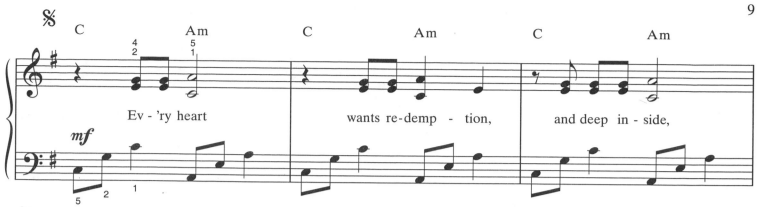

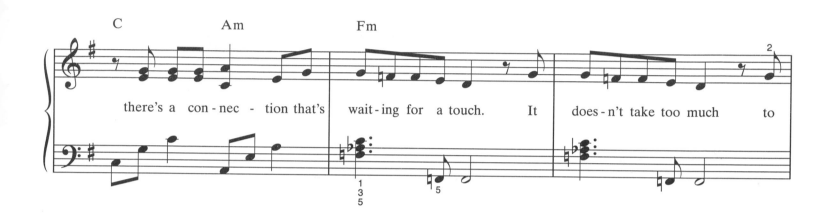

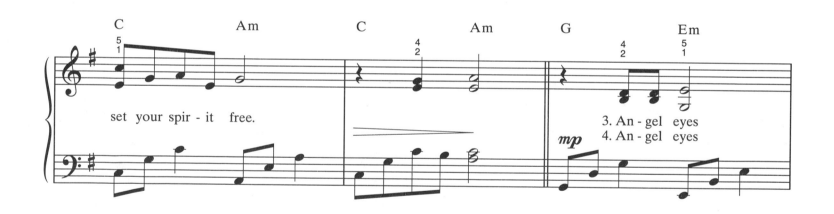

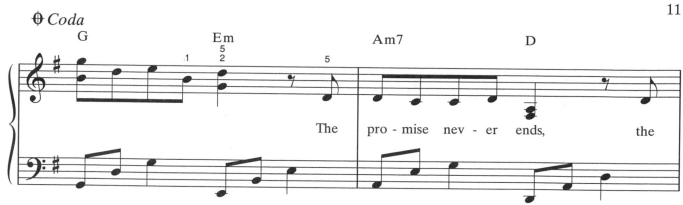

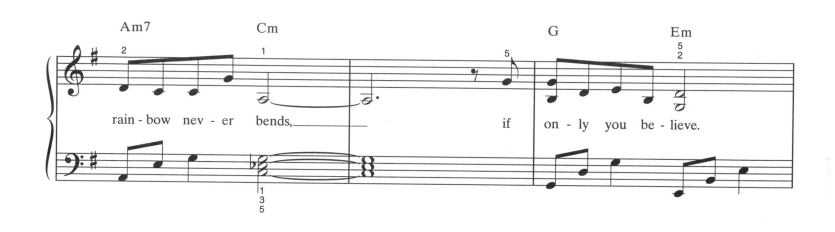

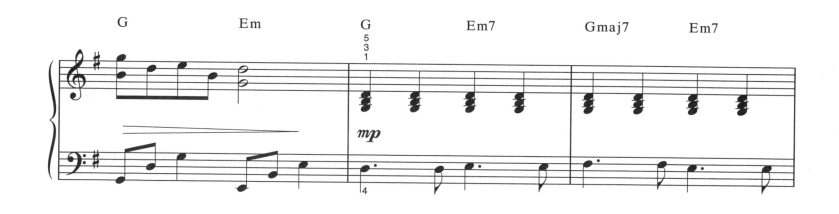

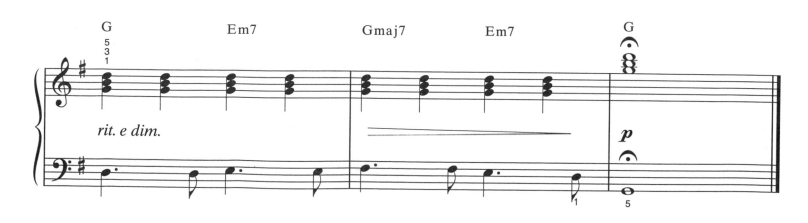

DUEL OF THE FATES

Music by
JOHN WILLIAMS
Arranged by DAN COATES

Maestoso, with great force

Kor - ah,_____ Mah - tah._____ Kor - ah,_____ Rah - tah-mah.

Allegro ♩ = 152

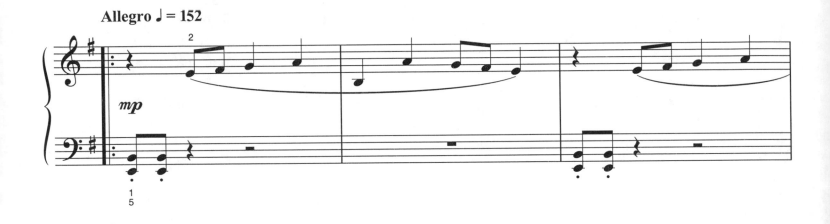

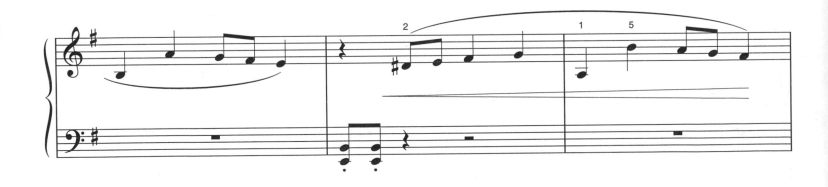

1.

Duel of the Fates - 5 - 1
AFM0304

14

FAWKES THE PHOENIX

Music by
JOHN WILLIAMS
Arranged by DAN COATES

Fawkes the Phoenix - 3 - 1
AFM0304

18

Fawkes the Phoenix - 3 - 3
AFM0304

GOLLUM'S SONG

as performed by Emiliana Torrini in the motion picture
"The Lord of the Rings: The Two Towers"

Words by FRAN WALSH
Music by HOWARD SHORE
Arranged by DAN COATES

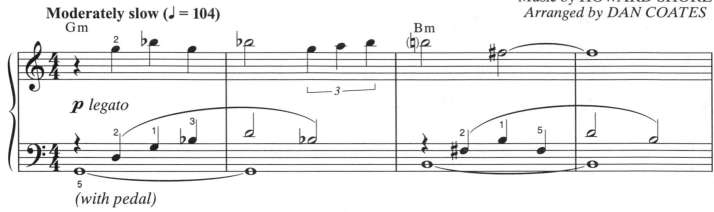

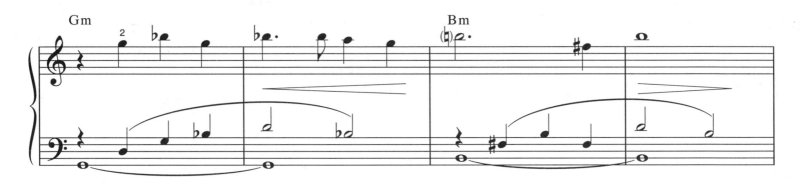

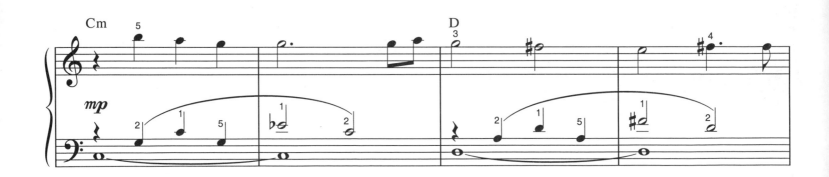

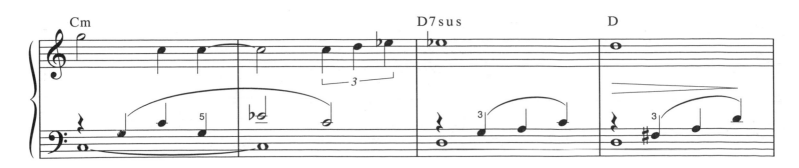

Gollum's Song - 4 - 1
AFM0304

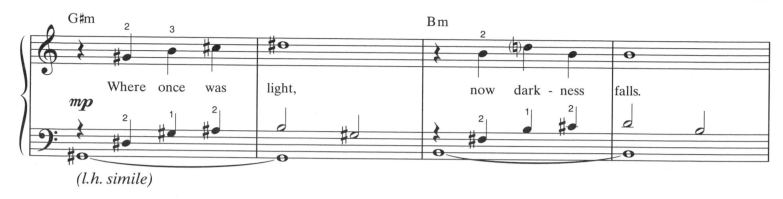

Where once was light,   now dark - ness falls.

(l.h. simile)

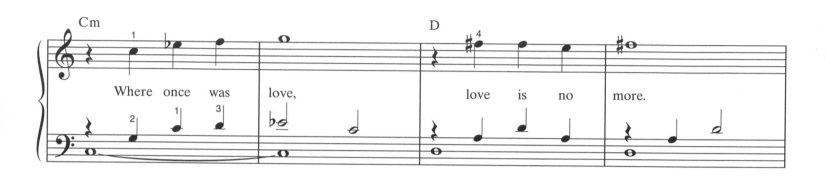

Where once was love,   love is no more.

Don't say good - bye.

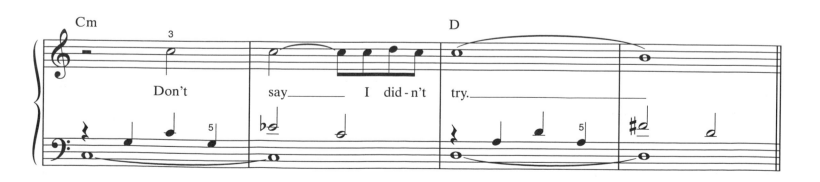

Don't say   I did - n't try.

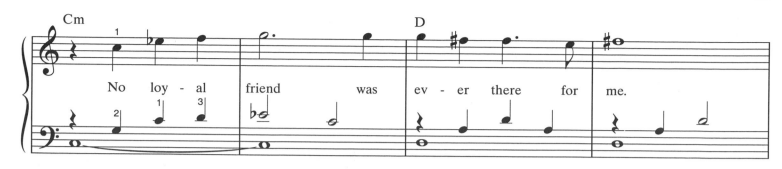

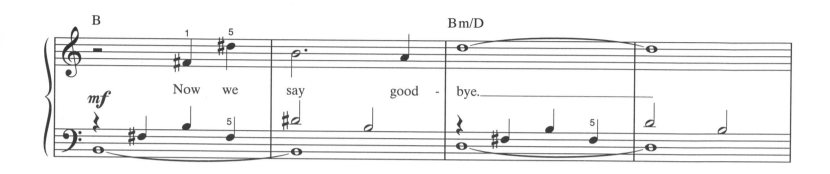

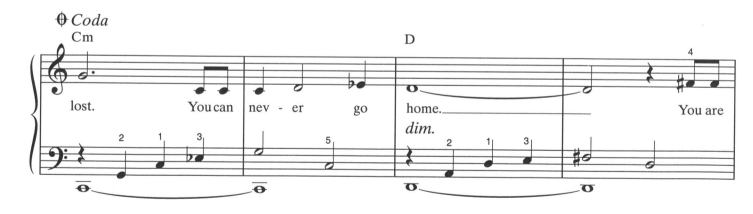

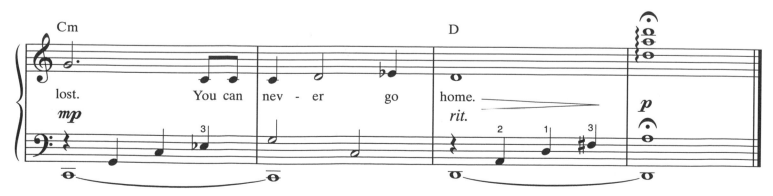

HARRY'S WONDROUS WORLD

Music by
JOHN WILLIAMS
Arranged by DAN COATES

Broadly (♩. = 60)

(with pedal throughout)

(♩ =108)

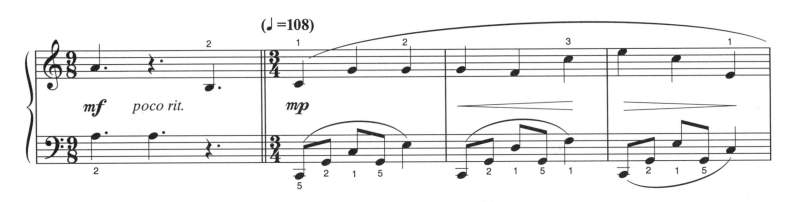

mf *poco rit.* *mp*

f

mf *simile*

Harry's Wondrous World - 4 - 1
AFM0304

HEDWIG'S THEME

Music by
JOHN WILLIAMS
Arranged by DAN COATES

Hedwig's Theme - 4 - 1
AFM0304

30

From the Columbia Pictures Motion Picture SPIDER-MAN

HERO

Words and Music by
CHAD KROEGER
Arranged by DAN COATES

Slowly (♩. = 48)

Verse 1:

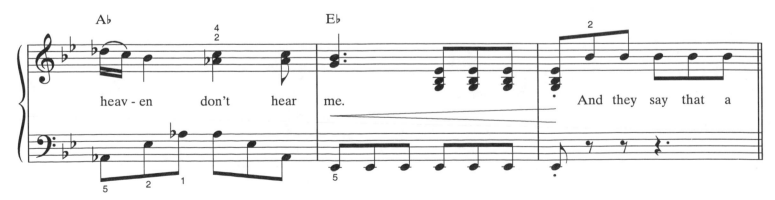

Hero - 5 - 1
AFM0304

Chorus:

he - ro could save us. I'm not gon - na stand here and wait. I'll hold on to the

wings of the ea - gles. Watch as we all fly a - way.

Verse 2:

2. Some - one told me____ love would all save us.____

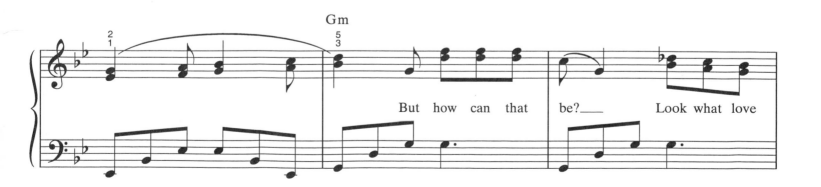

But how can that be?____ Look what love

gave us._____ A world full of kill-ing___ and blood

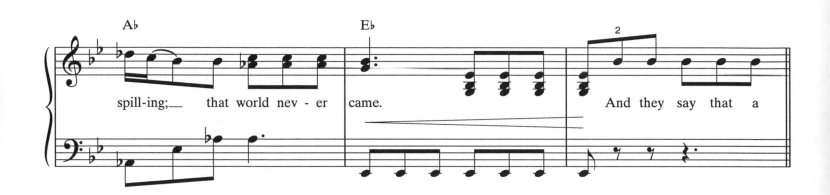

spill-ing;___ that world nev - er came. And they say that a

Chorus:

he - ro could save us. I'm not gon-na stand here and wait. I'll hold on to the

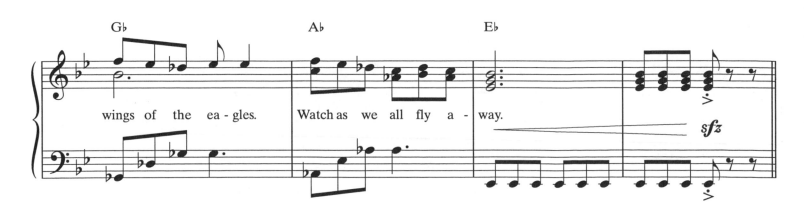

wings of the ea - gles. Watch as we all fly a - way.

I'M ALIVE

Words and Music by
KRISTIAN LUNDIN and ANDREAS CARLSSON
Arranged by DAN COATES

With a moderate, steady beat (♩ = 104)

Mmm. Mmm.

I get wings to fly, oh, I'm a - live.

When you

Chorus:

call on me, when I hear you breathe,

I'm Alive - 5 - 1
AFM0304

From the Motion Picture CHICAGO

I MOVE ON

Lyrics by
FRED EBB

Music by
JOHN KANDER
Arranged by DAN COATES

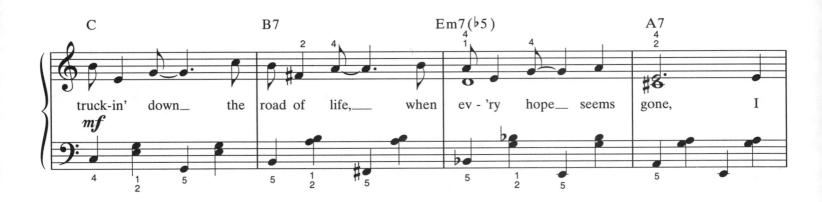

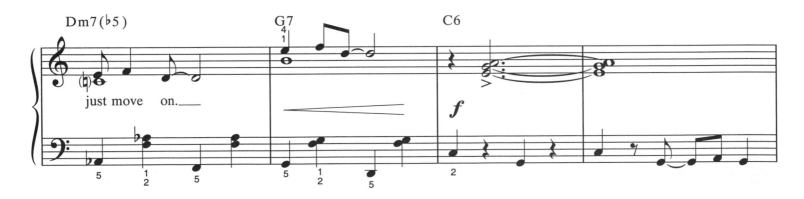

44

I Move On - 4 - 3
AFM0304

I'M NOT A GIRL,
NOT YET A WOMAN

Words and Music by
MAX MARTIN, RAMI
and DIDO ARMSTRONG
Arranged by DAN COATES

48

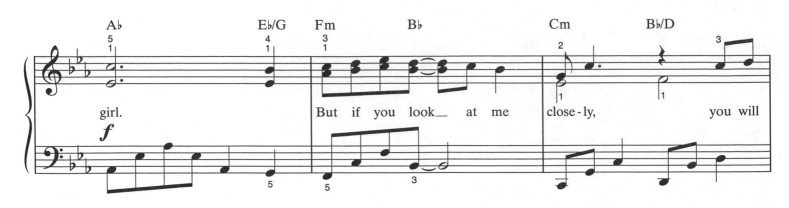

girl. But if you look at me close-ly, you will

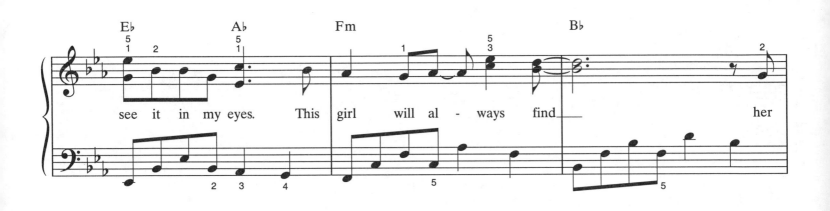

see it in my eyes. This girl will al-ways find her

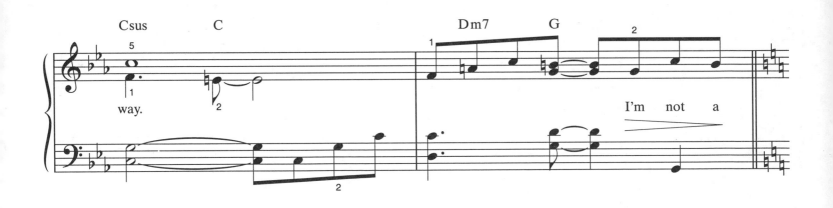

way. I'm not a

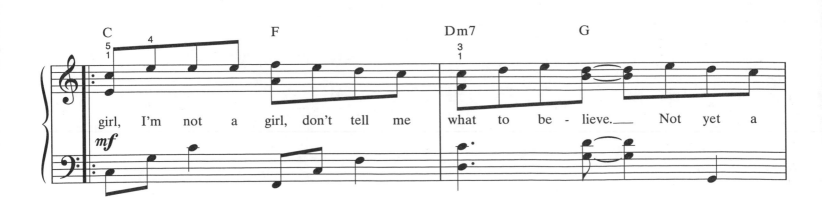

girl, I'm not a girl, don't tell me what to be-lieve. Not yet a

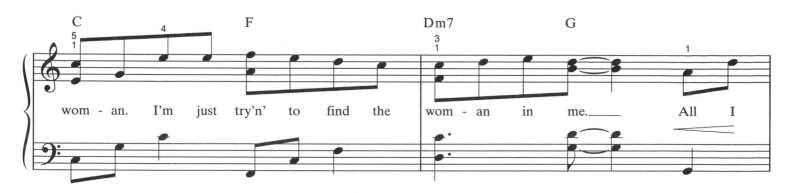

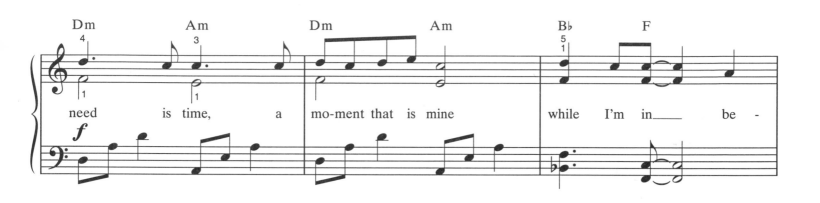

I'm Not a Girl, Not Yet a Woman - 4 - 4
AFM0304

IN DREAMS
(featured in "The Breaking Of The Fellowship")

Words and Music by
FRAN WALSH and
HOWARD SHORE
Arranged by DAN COATES

Slowly and freely

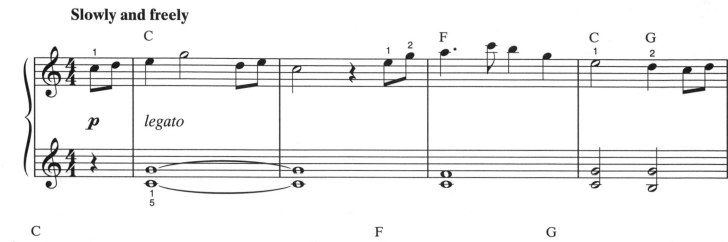

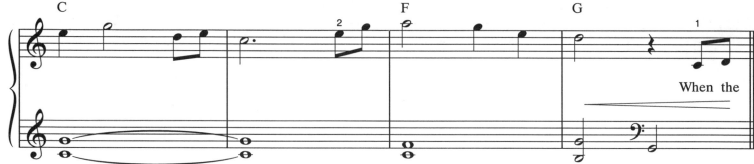

Moderately slow, flowing (♩ = 76)

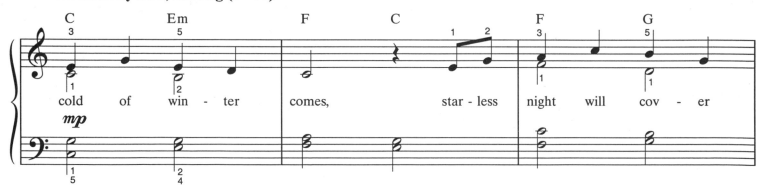

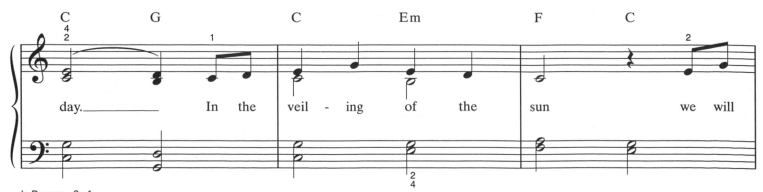

In Dreams - 3 - 1
AFM0304

walk_____ in bit-ter rain. But in dreams,_____ I can_____

hear_____ your name._____ And in dreams_____ we will_____

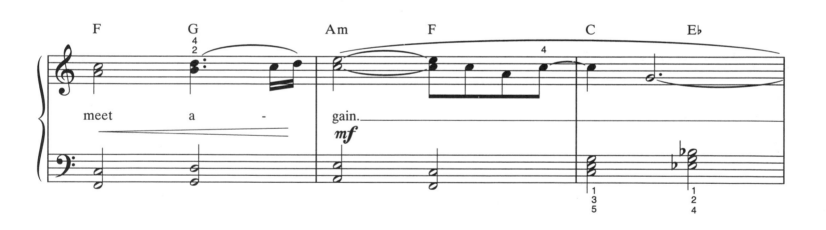

meet a - gain._____

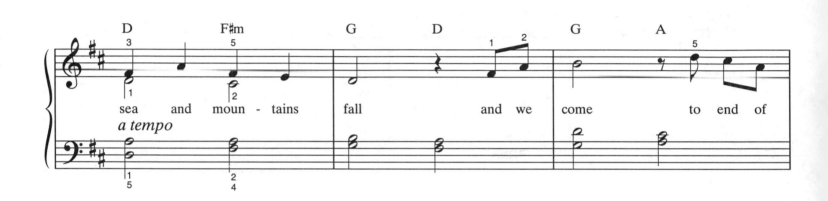

sea and moun - tains fall and we come to end of

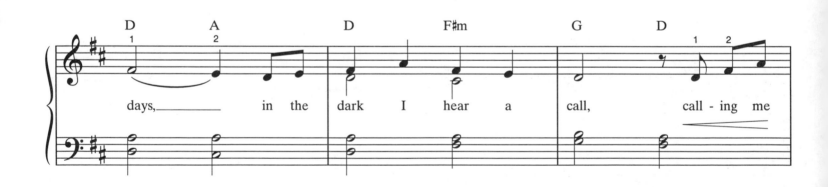

days,_____ in the dark I hear a call, call - ing me

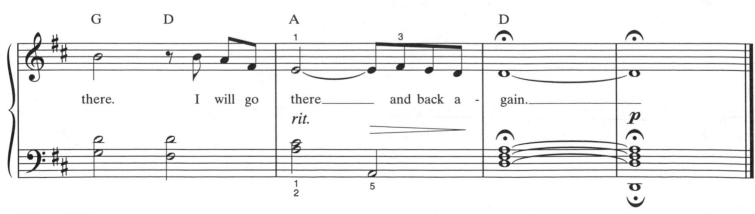

there. I will go there_____ and back a - gain._____

THE MEADOW PICNIC

Music by
JOHN WILLIAMS
Arranged by DAN COATES

The Meadow Picnic - 3 - 1
AFM0304

The Meadow Picnic - 3 - 3
AFM0304

JAMES BOND THEME

Music by
MONTY NORMAN
Arranged by DAN COATES

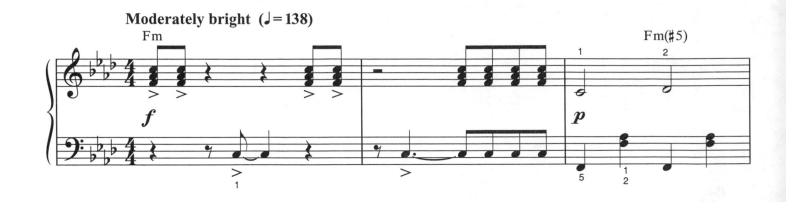

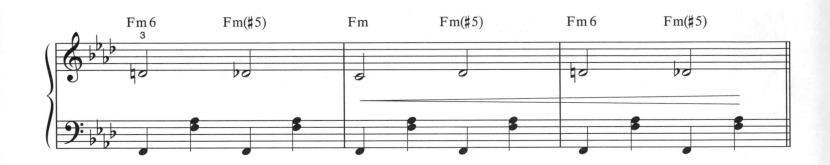

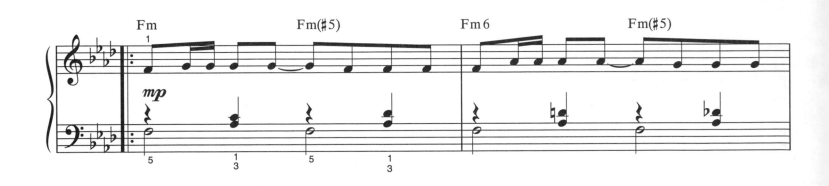

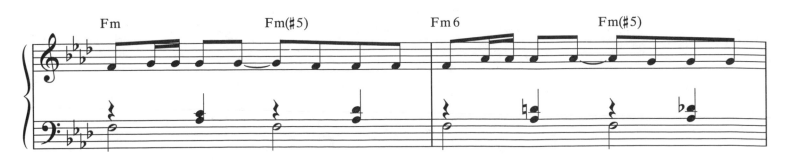

James Bond Theme - 4 - 1
AFM0304

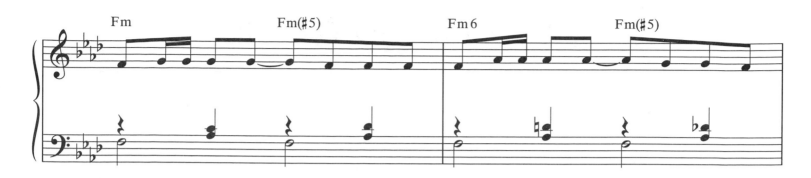

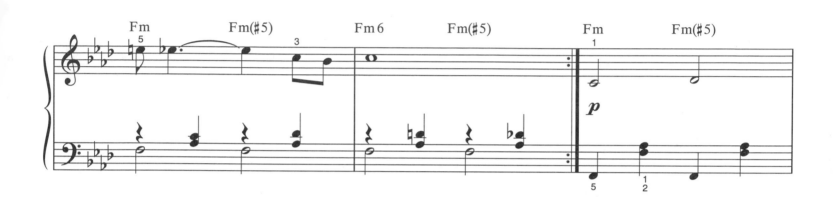

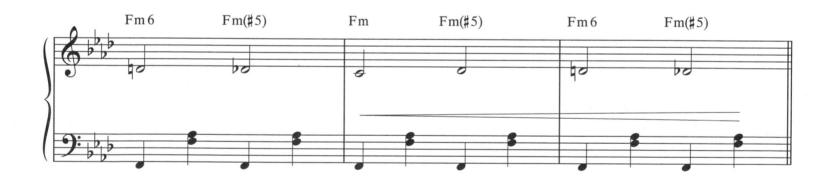

With a slight swing feeling

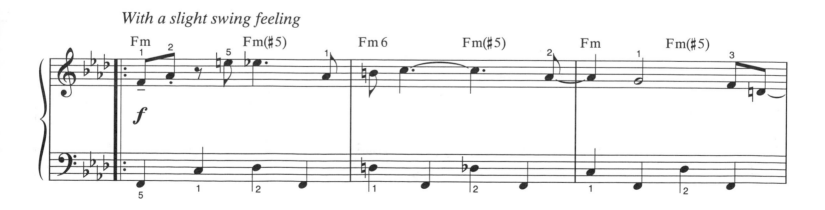

58

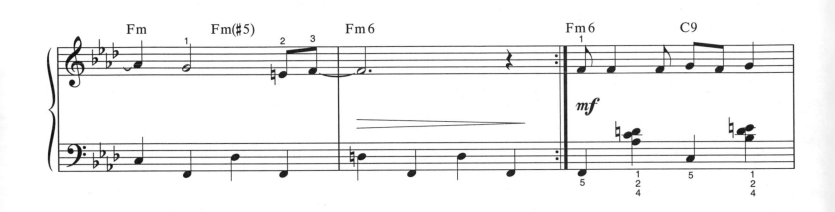

James Bond Theme - 4 - 3
AFM0304

MAY THE FORCE BE WITH YOU

Music by
JOHN WILLIAMS
Arranged by DAN COATES

THE PRAYER

Italian Lyric by
ALBERTO TESTA and TONY RENIS

Words and Music by
CAROLE BAYER SAGER and DAVID FOSTER
Arranged by DAN COATES

Slowly, with expression ♩ = 72

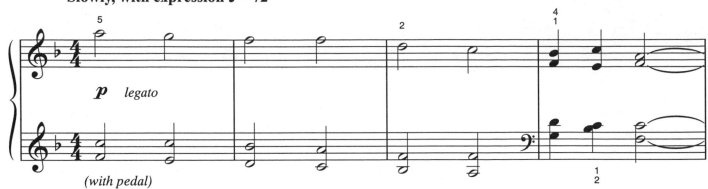

p legato

(with pedal)

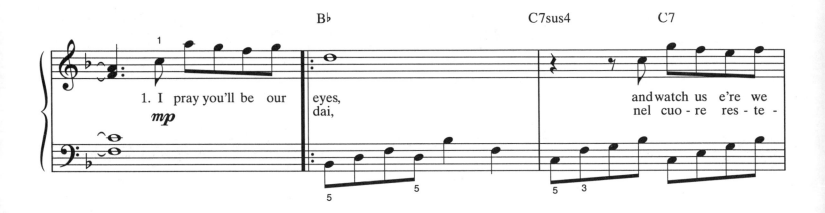

1. I pray you'll be our eyes,
dai,
mp

and watch us e're we
nel cuo - re res - te -

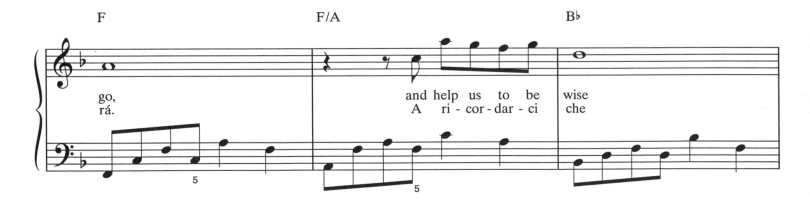

go,
rá.

and help us to be wise
A ri - cor - dar - ci che

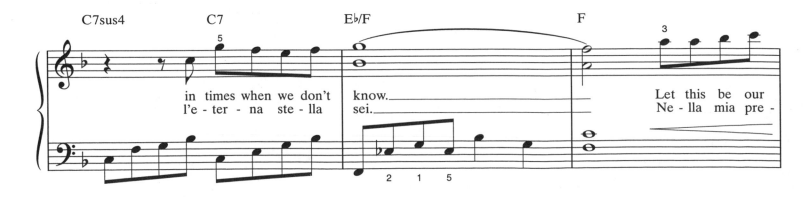

in times when we don't know.
l'e - ter - na ste - lla sei.

Let this be our
Ne - lla mia pre -

Verse 2: (English lyric):
I pray we'll find your light,
And hold it in our hearts
When stars go out each night.
Let this be our prayer,
When shadows fill our day.
Lead us to a place,
Guide us with your grace.
Give us faith so we'll be safe.

Verse 3 (Italian lyric):
La forza she ci dai
é il desiderio che.
Ognuno trovi amore
Intorno e dentro sé.
(Chorus:)

SOMEWHERE OUT THERE

Words and Music by
JAMES HORNER, BARRY MANN
and CYNTHIA WEIL
Arranged by DAN COATES

Somewhere out there beneath the pale moonlight, someone's think-in' of me and lov-ing me to-night. Somewhere

Somewhere Out There - 3 - 1
AFM0304

From Touchstone Pictures' "PEARL HARBOR"

THERE YOU'LL BE

Words and Music by
DIANE WARREN
Arranged by DAN COATES

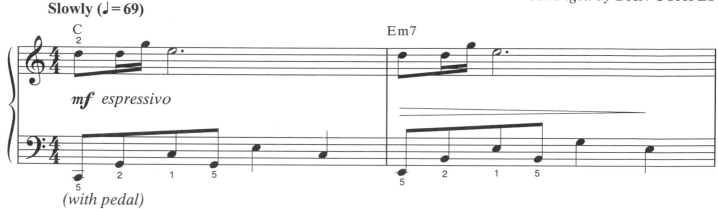

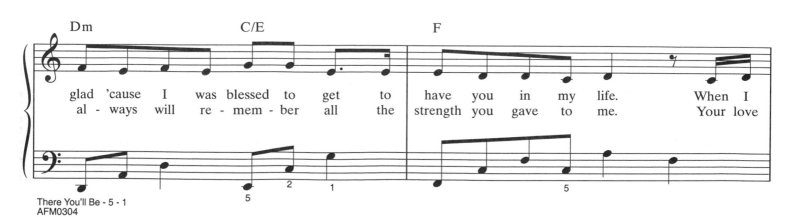

There You'll Be - 5 - 1
AFM0304

70

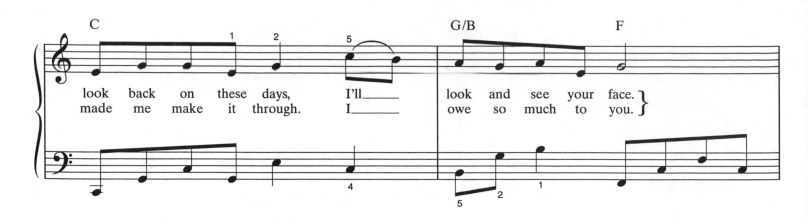

look back on these days, I'll____ look and see your face.
made me make it through. I____ owe so much to you.

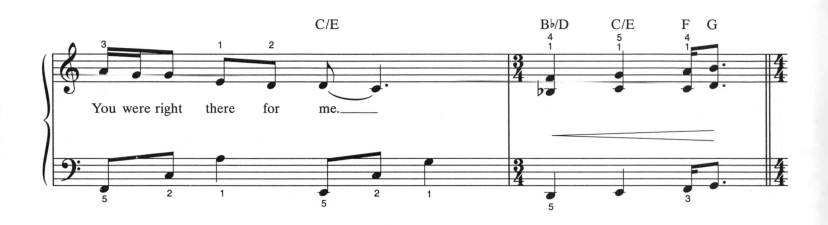

You were right there for me.____

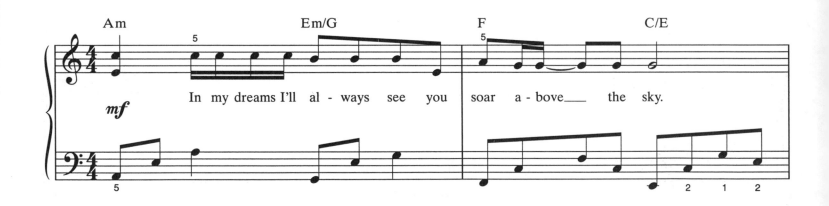

In my dreams I'll al - ways see you soar a - bove____ the sky.

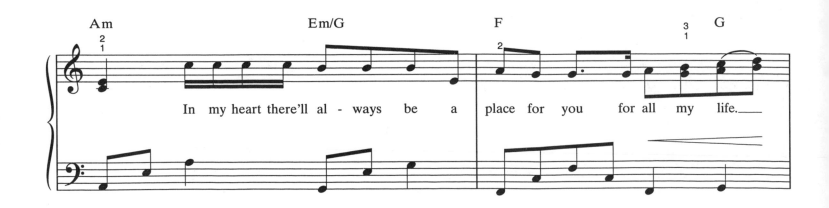

In my heart there'll al - ways be a place for you for all my life.____

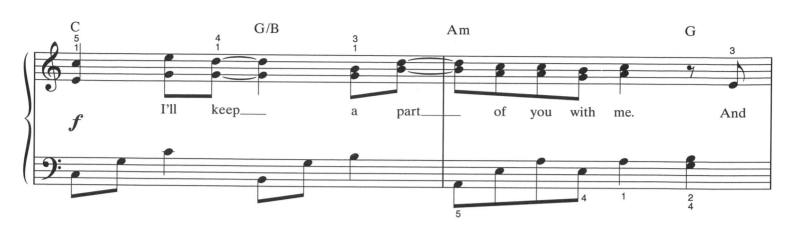

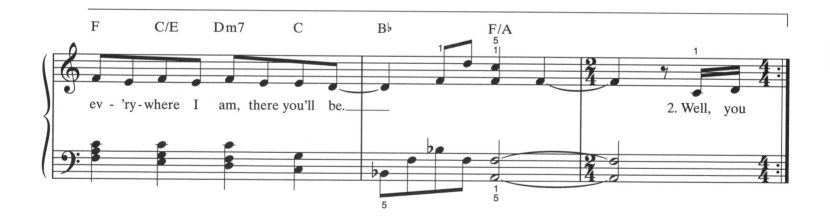

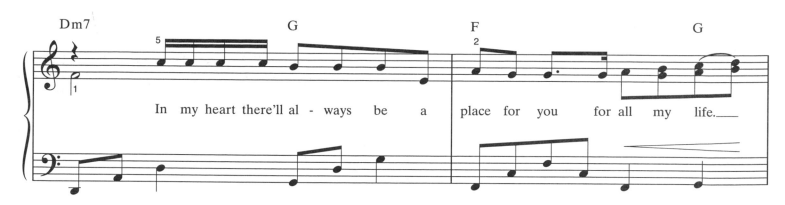

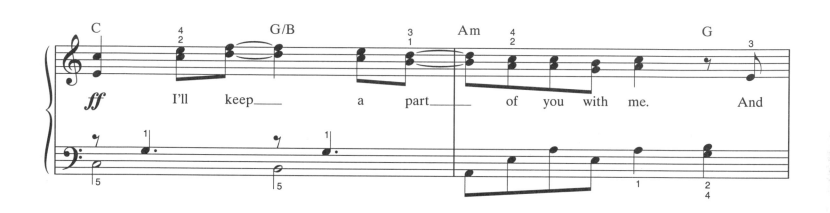

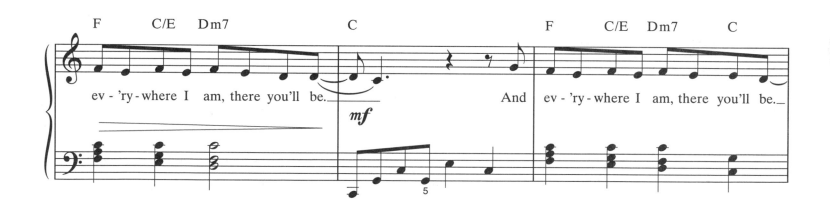

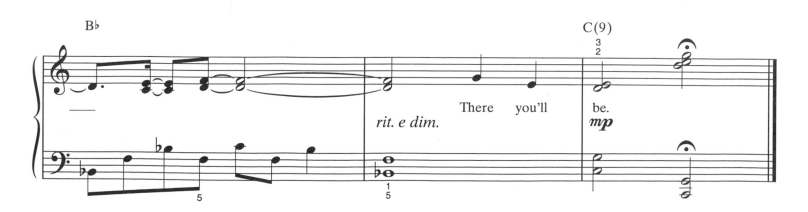

From the Twentieth Century-Fox Motion Picture "STAR WARS"

STAR WARS
(Main Title)

Music by
JOHN WILLIAMS
Arranged by DAN COATES

Majestically

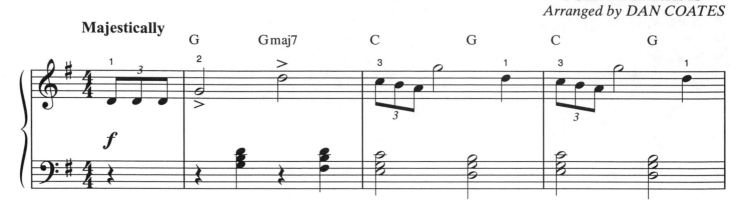

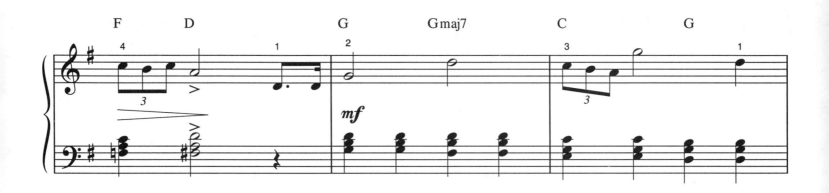

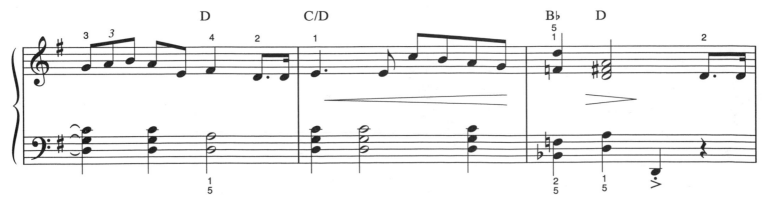

CAN'T FIGHT THE MOONLIGHT
(Theme from Coyote Ugly)

Words and Music by
DIANE WARREN
Arranged by DAN COATES

Moderate, steady beat (♩ = 98)

Verse:

1. Un-der a lov - er's sky, gon-na be___ with you, and no
2. There's no es - cape___ from love. Once the gen - tle breeze weaves

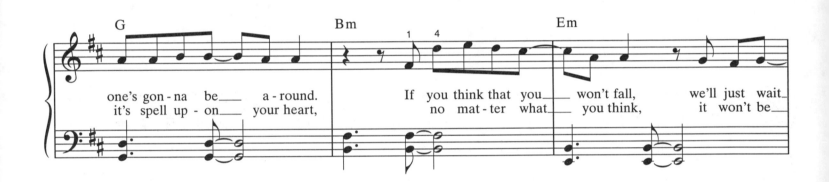

one's gon - na be___ a - round. If you think that you___ won't fall, we'll just wait
it's spell up - on___ your heart, no mat - ter what___ you think, it won't be

___ un - til, 'til the sun___ goes down.___ Un - der - neath___ the star-
___ too long 'til you're in___ my arms.___ Un - der - neath___ the star-

light, star - light,___ there's a mag - i - cal feel - ing so___ right.
light, star - light,___ we'll be lost___ in a rhy - thm so___ right.

Can't Fight the Moonlight - 4 - 1
AFM0304

Bridge:

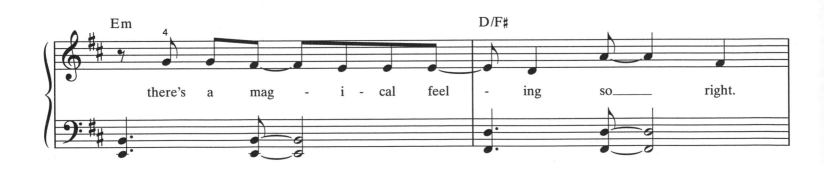

Chorus:

_ to re - sist,_ try to hide_ from my kiss,_ but you know,_ but you know_ that you

can't fight the moon - light. Deep_ in the dark,_ you'll sur - ren - der your heart. Don't you know,_

_ don't you know_ that you can't fight the moon - light, no, you can't fight_

_ it. You can try_ _ it. It's gon-na get to your heart._

New Series by Dan Coates!
Teacher's Choice!
Dan Coates Pop Keyboard Library

Designed to work with any piano method, this series offers an outstanding source of pedagogically sound supplementary material that is fun and exciting and will appeal to today's piano student. Specifically graded and with fingerings at each level, these books will expand any student's course of study, giving them incentive to practice and play more.

- The early levels (Books 1 and 2) have teacher accompaniment parts, and the titles have been carefully selected to appeal to the younger student (children's songs, patriotic music, folk songs, cartoon themes).

- Book 3 offers more pop titles, including music from *Harry Potter, Star Wars*, and even some Disney favorites.

- Books 4 and 5 (intermediate and advanced) cater to teen and adult players with great pop hits and standards, including the best movie themes and chart-topping pop ballads.

BOOK 1, Early Elementary
Titles are: America, the Beautiful • Little Sir Echo • The Merry-Go-Round Broke Down • On Top of Old Smokey • Take Me Out to the Ball Game • This Land Is Your Land • This Old Man • Twinkle, Twinkle, Little Star • When the Saints Go Marching In • The Yankee Doodle Boy.
(AFM0205)

BOOK 2, Mid-Elementary
Titles are: Jeopardy Theme • Lullaby and Goodnight • The Muffin Man • Ode to Joy (Theme from Beethoven's *Ninth Symphony*) • Over the Rainbow (from *The Wizard of Oz*) • She'll Be Coming 'Round the Mountain • The Song That Doesn't End • This Is It! (Theme from "The Bugs Bunny Show") • Today • You Are My Sunshine.
(AFM0206)

BOOK 3, Late Elementary
Titles are: Daisy, Daisy • (Meet) The Flintstones • Happy Wanderer • Harry's Wondrous World (from *Harry Potter and the Sorcerer's Stone*) • I Believe I Can Fly • I've Been Working on the Railroad • Somewhere Out There (from *An American Tail*) • Star Wars (Main Title) • Theme from *Ice Castles* (Through the Eyes of Love) • Theme from *Inspector Gadget* • Tomorrow • A Whole New World.
(AFM0207)

BOOK 4, Early Intermediate to Intermediate
Titles are: Candle in the Wind • Circle of Life • Hedwig's Theme (from *Harry Potter and the Sorcerer's Stone*) • I Hope You Dance • In Dreams (from *The Lord of the Rings*) • The James Bond Theme • The Pink Panther • Send in the Clowns • Somewhere My Love (from *Dr. Zhivago*) • Theme from *E.T. (The Extra-Terrestrial)* • To Love You More • Your Song.
(AFM0208)

BOOK 5, Late Intermediate to Advanced
Titles are: All By Myself • Amazed • Don't Cry for Me, Argentina (from *Evita*) • From This Moment On • The Prayer • Somewhere in Time • Somewhere Out There • Theme from *Schindler's List* • Time to Say Goodbye • Valentine.
(AFM0209)